SNOW AND ICE TECHNIQUES

Bill March

Revised by Bill Birkett

CICERONE PRESS
MILNTHORPE, CUMBRIA

© Bill March 1973, 1984
First published 1973 (As Modern Snow & Ice Techniques)
Reprinted 1974, 1975, 1976, 1977 (twice), 1979, 1980, 1983
Second (Revised Edition) 1984
Reprinted 1986, 1988
Third (Revised Edition) 1997

Cicerone Press,
2 Police Square,
Milnthorpe,
Cumbria, England

ISBN 1 85284 238 5

Cover illustration:
Dropline 5, New Hampshire
Photo: Bill Birkett

Printed by Carnmor Print & Design
95/97 London Road, Preston, Lancashire

SNOW AND ICE
TECHNIQUES

The author front pointing, picks hooking into ice.
Photo: John Cleare

CONTENTS

INTRODUCTION

The author's Introduction to the second edition is retained for its historical interest - Ed.

It is ten years since *Modern Snow and Ice Techniques* was written and developments have long outstripped the text, especially in the area of technical equipment. The impact of the ice revolution on the greater sport of mountaineering has been considerable. The ascent of vertical frozen waterfalls in Canada and the United States has added *The Ice Climbing Game* to Lito Tejada Flores' Classic concept of games climbers play. The impact has, however, been far greater than the development of a specialized area of expertise; the standard of mixed climbing has risen, alpine ascents are much faster and alpine Himalayan climbing has also fully utilized the new technology. Debates rage fiercely on the new ethics of ice climbing which the technology has raised, and climbers now focus on speed of ascent as their measure of technical competence and superiority over their peers. Although some of us may shake our heads in dismay or incomprehension at the cutting edge of the sport, it is the nature of men to compete and strive for greater accomplishments.

It was only a few decades ago that the use of crampons was frowned upon as unsportmanlike and only a decade ago that many British climbers laughed at John Cunningham's prancing on ice. Critics were soon silenced as the efficiency and boldness of the new technology proved its worth. Today the standard of ice climbing is extremely high with nearly all the classic Grade VI climbs in Canada being climbed in a day by virtually unknown young climbers. Youth does not suffer the psychological barriers breached by the early pioneers such as Cunningham, MacInnes and Chouinard but takes as the norm the accomplishments of the past.

There are some things which do not age and one of the most potent is the mountains themselves. Ten year ago, I wrote: 'It is important to remember that technical ability needs to be combined with a full appreciation of the constantly changing nature and attendant danger of the snow and ice environment. The latter ability can only be gained from personal experience in the mountains over a period of years'. That advice still holds good today. Perhaps one of the most thought provoking quotations I have come across in my climbing career is from a Farmers' Almanac - but it has powerful implications for the aspiring mountaineer: 'Good judgement is the result of experience - experience is the result of bad judgement'.

Good climbing!

Bill March, 1984

*Julie-Ann Clyma shows modern axe and crampons on the 1996
Changabang expedition (Courtesy Lyon Equipment Ltd)*

CHAPTER 1
THE ICE AXE

The climber must develop a feel for the mountains and be able to read them and understand them, selecting his route according to his needs and abilities, rather than insulating himself against the challenge *with a multitude of equipment* and a set of pre-conceived ideas.

The aspiring climber is faced with a bewildering assortment of ice axes and hammers to choose from in today's technological age. The first question to ask oneself when buying an ice axe is, 'What do I want it for: alpine climbing and glacier travel, or north walls and waterfall climbing?' The alpine mountaineer requires an axe for cutting steps, for self-arrest, for support on steep ground, for probing crevasses and, in some cases, for belaying, although this latter function is better performed using a deadman anchor. The waterfall climber requires an axe primarily as a 'hook in' handhold and a super-strong shaft is not as important a requirement as weight/balance/resilience and feel. However, where the axe or hammer is used as a back-up 'hooked in' anchor the overall shaft/head attachment strength is also important.

Wood Shafts
Ash and hickory shafts are now regarded as obsolete, although a good straight grained hickory shaft is light, has minimum vibration, is warm to hold and a 'good feel'. Laminated bamboo is stronger than hickory, but more expensive. Wood shafts can be re-inforced with glass fibre wraps, but this makes for a heavier axe.

Fibre Glass
Glass fibre and carbon filament reinforced plastic shafts are available with the space age technology and there are strong, light weight shafts available. It is important, however, to be aware of variation in material strength with low temperatures.

Metal Shafts
Aluminium and titanium shafts are becoming increasingly popular in spite of their lack of reliance and tendency to jar the wrist when hooking or cutting on hard ice. They are, however, very strong and well attached to the head, ferrule and spike. Metal axes have a tendency to be cold, i.e., they conduct heat away from the hands.

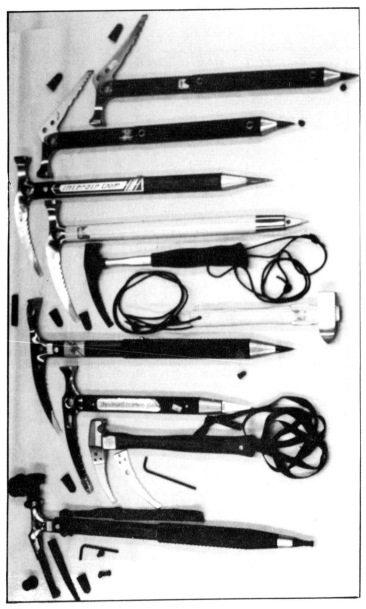

This can be a serious problem when waterfall climbing at low temperatures with the hands above the head for long periods. To some extent, the provision of thick moulded rubber or neoprene grips has decreased the problem of jarring and cold conduction, and many climbers are now using metal shafted axes because of their strength.

Length

The length of the axe is always the subject of much debate, but the following may be taken as a general guide: Alpine climbing, 70 cms for the average person - a rough guide is if the axe head is held in the hand down by the side of the body, the spike should just touch the ground. Waterfall/Gully climbing/North Faces, 50-60cms for the average person - a rough guide, the shaft not including the ferrule and spike, should be the distance from elbow to finger tip. At the present time, I personally prefer 55cm, which is longer than I used in Scotland. I find the longer length better for reaching over bulges, fewer placements are required, there is less likelihood of knuckles hitting ice; greater leverage is available when placing and removing ice screws; and more security provided when mantel-shelfing on the inserted shaft in soft snow.

Cross Section

The cross section of the shaft is an important consideration as the flattened oval gives a more secure grip and better control of pick direction than the more rounded shafts. Ribbing on the rubber

Left:
Ice tools of the early 1970's
reflect a search for the definitive shape.

moulded handle greatly improves the grip. The hand grip is especially important for ice climbers who may be hanging on the axe for long periods.

Head: Pick and Adze

The heads of ice axes are now made of high quality steel, e.g. chrome molybdenum, chrome vanadium. There are two schools of thought, one favouring heavy heads to give weight to the placement or cut and the other favouring light heads, reducing the carrying weight, but increasing the physical effort of placement and cutting, especially in hard ice.

The design of the pick varies according to the type of work it is required to do. There are three basic pick designs: (1) the curved pick, (2) the inclined pick and (3) the banana or 'dished pick' which is really a composite design of one and two. The conventional curved pick is the most widespread design and it provides a hooking action in snow and ice which is useful in emergency self-arrest. The standard alpine axe should have a curve of 65-70 degrees whilst a waterfall axe should have a curve of 55-60 degrees to give better purchase on vertical ice walls. The essentials of pick design for an ice climbing axe are:

1. The curve of the pick is co-incident to the axis of the arm to ensure maximum penetration.

2. A thin wall tapered pick giving greater penetration and vibration. Not too thin as it may have a tendency to stick or be structurally weakened.

3. A set of teeth cut into the underside of the pick at the tip to prevent it slipping out.

Right:
A selection of Charlet-Moser ice tools
(Courtesy Lyon Equipment Ltd)

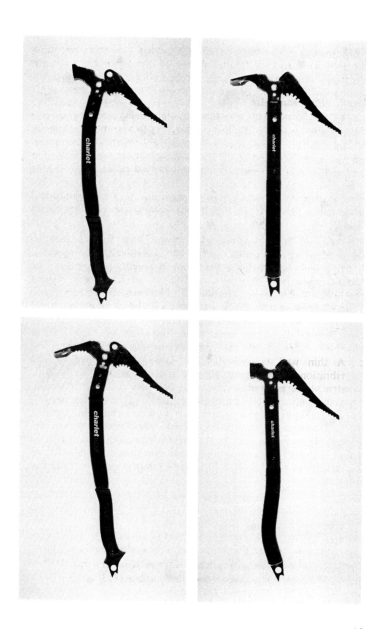

When using a 55-60 degree pick for cutting steps there may be a tendency for it to stick. This can be avoided by cutting in a straight line rather than a curve. There are axes especially designed for cutting with thicker picks and abrupt tapers and no notches, which shatter the ice on impact. The question of the angle of contact of the cutting edge of the pick on the ice has raised the question of positive and negative clearance of the ice pick, (see diagram). It is maintained by some that positive clearance is required for effective self-arrest on ice, but since self-arrest on ice is virtually impossible and I have used axes with a negative clearance on numerous occasions for effective self-arrest, I regard this as a non-issue. However, when self-arresting with a dropped curve, you will encounter a strong rotational movement which may pull the shaft from your grip if it is not held securely.

In contrast to the curved pick, there is an inclined pick or Terrordactyl which juts down at 55°/60° to the shaft. This requires a different technique and is placed with more of a pulling down or hooking action. On steep ice, the original models tended to cut a pocket in which it hooked after two or three blows. The inclined pick is easier to extract than the curved pick, although it has a less natural placement action. When used in conjunction with a short shaft on hard fluted ice, there were many instances of 'Terrordactyl Knuckles' suffered by the over enthusiastic ice climber. The innovative American ice climber, Jeff Lowe has developed the tube pick or Humming Bird ice hammer and eventually the Big Bird, which is an ice axe with a tube pick. The tube pick is excellent on brittle ice, giving a secure purchase and allowing the climber to pivot the shaft. Since the pick rotates this greatly facilitates traversing moves. However, the tube pick has a tendency to stick in normal ice, hold poorly in wet ice, and should not be used as a lever to extract ice screws as it may break. It is a good example of a highly specialized tool developed for the often brittle low temperature ice of vertical waterfalls.

Right:
Top: The CAMP Hyper-Couloir system is the updated version of the first fully exchangeable pick system which was pioneered by CAMP.
Below: The CAMP Woodpecker (Courtesy Allcord Ltd)

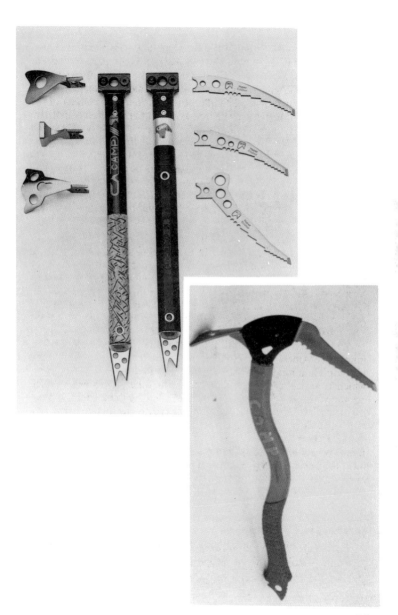

15

The Banana Pick was originally developed from the ice pick of the Forrest Mjollnir hammer which was dished on its upper pick surface in a banana shape. This design was incorporated eventually into the Forrest Lifetime axe and had teeth all the way along the bottom edge of the pick. The banana pick gives excellent placement and ease of removal with minimum occurrence of sticking in the ice. The upper dished surface facilitates extraction allowing the pick to be removed by levering the axe shaft away from the ice surface. The banana, or reverse curve, pick is generally the best tool for climbing steep snow or ice. A slightly longer pick design also reduces the possibility of Terrordactyl knuckles.

The debate on pick design is rendered somewhat redundant by the development of interchangeable picks, an innovation pioneered by Bill Forrest and followed by Lowe Alpine Systems in the U.S.A. and several European equipment manufacturers. The climber can choose almost any type of pick to suit his inclination.

The Adze

The design of the adze depends on the curves; the forward curve and the transverse curve. The forward curve of the adze from the shaft head should coincide with the arc of cutting to give a smooth unimpeded action. The traverse course should be slight or non-existent, as a scooped edge has a tendency to catch on the corner of the step being cut. The tubular adze is found on the Lowe Alpine Systems. Big Bird is also effective in cutting snow and ice since all the force is directed into the centre of the tube and the ice extruded out by each successive blow. A sharp conventional adze can be used to cut ice but if it is thick with a sharp taper on the cutting edge, it will shatter and spray ice fragments on the step cutter's face.

Ferrule and Spike

The ferrule and spike should be firmly attached to the shaft and should be streamlined to facilitate sensitive probing for crevasses. The spike should be flat in the same plane as the pick of the axe and should have a karabiner eye hole if it is to be used for waterfall ice climbing.

Ice Hammer/North Wall Hammer

The ice hammer is basically an ice axe, without a ferrule and spike, which has the adze replaced by a hammer head. The north wall hammer is similar to an ice hammer excepting that the ferule and spike are retained and it is the desired tool for the double axe technique in alpine climbing. All of the design features mentioned in ice axes apply to ice hammer/north wall axes with the proviso that the

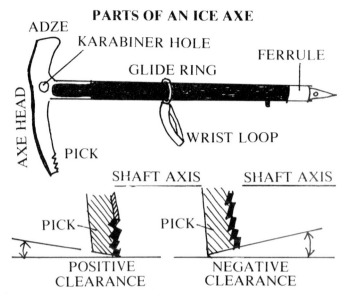

PARTS OF AN ICE AXE

ADZE

KARABINER HOLE

GLIDE RING

FERRULE

AXE HEAD

PICK

WRIST LOOP

SHAFT AXIS

SHAFT AXIS

PICK

PICK

POSITIVE
CLEARANCE

NEGATIVE
CLEARANCE

length of the hammer tends to be less than 65cm. The hammer is essential for placing drive-in ice pitons, rock pitons and bolt anchors, all of which may be used in a variety of ice climbing situations.

Maintenance of Equipment
The ice axe and ice hammer are the ice climber's tools and as such should be kept sharp at all times. It is important to sharpen equipment along the original design lines of the factory fresh tools although inevitably with wear there will be some smoothing down. A file rather than a powered grindstone should be used since the latter may overheat and destroy the temper of the cutting edge of the metal. On long mixed routes it may be useful to carry a small file for re-sharpening tools blunted by rock.

All gear should be checked for fatigue cracks and hairline fractures before climbs since they are subject to considerable stress and a failure could prove fatal. Exposed metal parts should be protected with a thin film of oil to prevent rust, and sharp edges should be protected by leather sheaths or rubber bungs whichever is appropriate. Adjustable tools should be checked frequently to ensure that all screws and any other adjustment nuts are securely tightened.

SHORT SLING ATTACHED TO
AXE HEAD AND WOUND
AROUND THE SHAFT WITH
LOOP IN INSIDE OF PALM

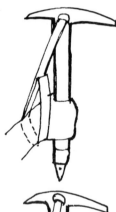

SHORT SLING WITH LOOP
ON OUTSIDE OF WRIST

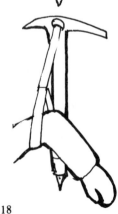

THE ARM STRAP HANG
FOR RESTING WRIST AND
FOREARMS

Ice Axe Attachments

This subject has been heavily debated especially with the emergence of a nascent code of ice climbing ethics along the lines of high standard rock climbing. The distinction must first be made between alpine ice climbing and waterfall ice climbing which are in some respects technically different. Secondly, the function of the attachment cord must be defined: attachment may be used for the following: Safety, Support, Resting, Aid.

(i) SAFETY

- To avoid dropping the axe or hammer; in this instance the ice tool may be attached to the body by a long sling, or a sliding wrist loop/short sling to wrist, or carried in a holster at the hip with no sling. It is really a matter of opinion which one you adopt although it is generally agreed that novices should have some form of ice axe attachment. The following table summarizes the pros and cons of different methods and the reader can draw his own conclusions.

1.   Sliding Wrist Loop/Short Sling to Wrist.

Cons:	a) Danger of injury if you fall and lose a grip of your axe.
	b) Awkward to change from hand to hand.
	c) Dangles and gets in the way when free climbing.
	d) Sliding wrist clasp places axe head near hand and could affect compass navigation.
Pros:	a) Attached to wrist and easily at hand.
	b) Gives some support to wrist when cutting or hooking.

2.   Long Sling to Body.

Cons:	a) Danger of injury if you fall and lose grip of your axe.
	b) Tangles up easily on equipment.
Pros:	a) Attached to body.
	b) Can be used to hang on for resting/back up anchor.
	c) Can be changed from hand to hand.

3. Holster.
   Cons: a) Could drop axe.
          b) Awkward for long alpine axes.
   Pros: a) Easily accessible.
          b) Completely and easily mobile from hand to hand.

(ii) SUPPORT

-Where the wrist loop is used to give support to the climber's grip when he is cutting on alpine ice or hanging in 'piolet traction' on steep waterfall ice. The wrist loop should be of 1″ tape since rope or ½″ tape cuts into the wrist, is uncomfortable, and can cut off the circulation to the hands. There are several different ways of using the short wrist loop as shown in the diagrams and I recommend the reader experiment and adopt the method he feels most comfortable with. Some climbers use the wrist loop as an arm strap hang for resting, in this instance the wrist loop needs to be large enough to admit a clothed forearm. The wrist loop can be used for resting by hanging on fully extended arms with the hands in the wrist loops, at the same time relaxing your grip on the shafts of the ice tools.

(iii) RESTING

- Here a long sling attachment or umbilical cord (sometimes adjustable) attaches from the ice tool to the climber's harness. The climber places the tool and rests his body weight on the sling whilst recovering his arm strength, placing a screw, or warming his hands. The length of the sling attachment is critical - too long and the climber will not be able to reach the ice tool; too short and his upward range of extension and placement will be curtailed. The optimum length I use is a sling which allows full vertical extension of the climber's arm to obtain the maximum distance apart of tool placements. Another method of resting is to use a fifi hook on a short cow's tail and hook it onto the wrist loop of the climbing tool placed above you. Strictly speaking, in the modern ethical sense many climbers regard resting as a form of aid climbing. All forms of ice climbing today have an element of aid and it is really up to the individual climber to make decisions on his own style of ascent since it is his life he is playing with.

(iv) AID

- One form of aid climbing peculiar to ice is where etriers are attached to the ice tools for steep overhanging ice. This method involves the climber placing the ice tool and standing in the etrier then placing the second ice tool and stepping up into the second etrier. This takes the weight off his front points and onto his insteps reducing the effort required. This technique was used in some of the early ascents of the vertical waterfall ice climbs in the Canadian Rockies but has now virtually disappeared from use.

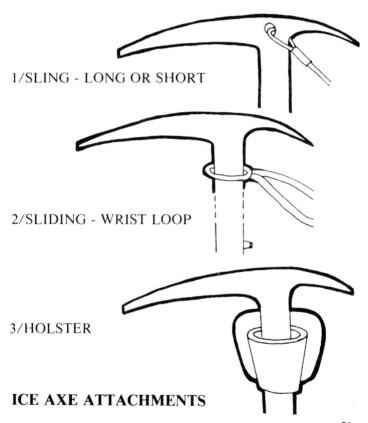

1/SLING - LONG OR SHORT

2/SLIDING - WRIST LOOP

3/HOLSTER

ICE AXE ATTACHMENTS

CHAPTER 2
CRAMPONS

There are almost as many types of crampons as there are ice axes and one has a problem in selecting a suitable pair. Crampons should be light, strong and adjustable with a secure fastening to the climbing boot. The original crampon had 10 downward projecting points but this has been replaced by the 12 point crampon with two additional front points or lobster claws projecting from the toe of the boot. The choice between a rigid crampon and a flexible or hinged crampon is a personal one although one should note the following points:

(i)   Rigid crampons have a greater tendency to ball up in soft snow conditions than hinged crampons.

(ii) Rigid crampons do appear to suffer from metal fatigue and cracks and breaks have occurred in all the rigid models I have used in my personal climbing.

(iii) Rigid crampons are claimed to vibrate less and give a more positive placement.

From my own experience I have found the flexible hinged crampon securely fastened to the new rigid plastic climbing boots to be adequate for the hardest ice climbs.

Right:
CRAMPONS - Standard crampons (top) are still popular. The lightweight crampons (centre) are mainly for trekking, rather than serious climbing. The rigid-frame step-in crampons are for technical ice climbing.   (Courtesy Allcord Ltd)

23

Design/Fitting of Crampons

The fitting of crampons is a skilled task and great care should be taken to fit the crampons snuggly to the boot welt.

1. Crampons should always be fitted to full shank rigid boots.

2. The crampon should have tangs (uprights) of an adequate length to grip the boot welt and should be sprung fit with the wire back bar firmly clipped over the welt of the heel.

3. The front points should project ¾″ - 1″ beyond the toe of the boot for vertical ice climbing. This distance is accurately measured by placing a piece of thin cardboard vertically across the toe of the boot and measuring the protrusion of the front points.

4. The front points should incline at 45° downwards and may be in a straight or curved plane. The wide bearing surface of the front point is best in the horizontal plane - crampons with the widest dimension in the vertical plane have a tendency to shear out of soft ice. Some crampons have the first set of downward projecting points behind the front points inclined forward at an angle so that when the climber drops his heel they contact the ice giving stability and support. I personally favour downward projecting points behind my front points since it facilitates mixed climbing moves and with sharp front points penetration is deep enough to allow support from the points behind. A further development has been wider spacing of the front points which again enhances stability but greatly increases the likelihood of snagging and tripping. These 'cow catcher' crampons are potentially very dangerous and I would not recommend them for all round mountaineering.

Fastening the Crampon to the Boot

The most efficient crampon strap is one of neoprene coated nylon used with the conventional buckle attachment. This does not freeze up, is strong and flexible and provides a secure positive attachment when used with a buckle. The original crampon strap was one long strap threaded through all the tangs and secured with a buckle on the outside of the heel. Crampon buckles are always fastened on the outside of the heel to reduce the chance of snagging or tripping on a protruding buckle. The most popular system now is to use four straps - two on the front four tangs and two on the rear two tangs (see diagram). The front straps may be locked by threading through the outside of the rings and twisting under and over the front toe strap. An even faster system which avoids threading any tang rings is to fasten two of the front tang straps together on a key ring and thread the inside strap through the ring to the outside buckle (see diagram). Straps should be fastened firmly but not so tight as to restrict circulation. The new rigid plastic climbing boots have a rigid upper shell which greatly reduces this problem. There are several spring clip methods of fastening crampons like ski bindings which are faster than the conventional strap method. (Often known as step-in crampons and now the accepted standard fastening.)

Pros and Cons of Crampons
The great advantage of crampons is the mobility they bestow on the climber - he is able to climb up, down, across, diagonally without cutting steps. This advantage outweighs all the disadvantages listed below.

(i)   There are 24 sharp points which may injure you or your companion in a slip or a fall.

(ii) There is a danger of tripping and snagging the crampons on the instep. It is important to wear close fitting gaiters to reduce the risk of this occurring.

(iii) Under certain conditions, i.e. damp snow, the crampons ball up and become dangerous *'sabots de neige'*. The side of the boot must be sharply tapped with the ferrule of the axe to release the accumulation of snow. A layer of plastic tape or nylon coated cloth on the base of the crampon reduces the likelihood of 'balling up'.

(iv) They require practice and training to use them properly. On inexperienced feet they are more of a hindrance than a help.

(v)   They can be difficult on mixed ground, especially fields, as it is akin to walking on mini stilts and ankles can be twisted on small rocks.

(vi) In a fall they tend to cartwheel the climber end over end.

Care and Maintenance of Crampons
Crampons should always be kept sharp for ice climbing and the adjusting nuts should be checked frequently and re-tightened as necessary. Never use a power grindstone when sharpening crampons as you may destroy the temper. When sharpening points - sharpen downward projecting points on their edges to a chisel point and the

CRAMPON FASTENINGS

RT. BOOT

4 STRAP

1. Back Strap Buckle
2. Back Strap double wrap for support
3. Front Strap Buckle
4. Front Strap overlapped at A & B to lock toe straps

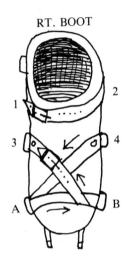

RT. BOOT

4 STRAPS WITH RING FASTENER ATTACHMENT

1. As above
2. As above
3. Front Strap Buckle looped through ring X
4. ⎰ Staps all
5. ⎱ linked to
6. ⎰ ring X

(N.B. Modern step-in crampons have largely superseded strap crampons.)

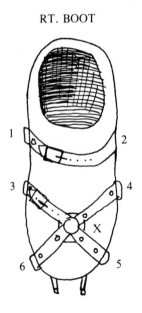

front points on the top to a chisel edge. A thin smear of oil will keep them from rusting and in good condition. Since most modern crampons are made from high tensile steel alloys, e.g. Chrome Molybdenum, it is important to check for hairline fractures and fatigue cracks after heavy usage especially if you have been mixed climbing. The straps, buckles and rivets of the bindings should also be thoroughly checked for wear and tear and malfunction.

Crampon Technique

At the present time there are three so called different crampon techniques.

1. The French technique, flat footed or *pied à plat,* utilizing the downward pointing spikes on the base of the feet. This is used on slopes up to 65° and requires flexible and diligent practice to master on the steeper slopes.

2. The German technique, front pointing or *pied en avant,* utilizing the forward pointing spikes at the front of the crampons. This is used on the steeper slopes up to the vertical and requires strong calf muscles.

3. The American technique or *pied à trois,* which is the combination of the two techniques.

The first basic principle in crampon technique is to utilize the points of the crampons at right angles to the ice surface for maximum purchase. Although the above terms are useful in learning, the ideal is to have a free style of cramponing where one can alternate from front point to bottom points and vice versa fluidly and easily whenever the occasion demands. It should be remembered that front pointing is effective on low angle ice especially when the heel can be raised with the knees in contact with the ice in a resting position. The second principle in cramponing is 'centering' - this involves maintaining the body mass centred over the positioned feet in stable balance when motionless. When the climber wishes to move his right foot he centres his body weight over his left foot in a position of balance. This is crucial to sound crampon technique since the body weight is directly over the support crampon, in balance, and pushing the points into the ice whilst the free foot is in movement. Once the foot is placed the body weight is centred between the two feet. It is important not to take too big a step and overextend the centering movement. The third principle in crampon technique is to develop rhythm, spring and crisp efficient weight transfer. It is useful when practising to exaggerate the movement and emphasize the putting down of the feet firmly to ensure good penetration of the crampon points. Complete weight transfer from one foot to the other combined with a 'cat like spring' is required to develop this technique.

There are three basic foot positions in the French technique:

1. Walking - *'marche' normal;* flat footed walk in any direction up, down and across. 0-15 degrees.

2. Duck walk *'en canard';* walking with the feet splayed out and sitting back so the weight is over the crampons. Walk up and down facing out using this technique. 15-30 + degrees.

3. Flat footed - *pied à plat;* facing out. 30-60 degrees.

The ice axe plays an important role in the practice of the *pied à plat* technique and the following table gives the axe positions for the different slope angles:

Piolet Canne	30-40° Easy	Vertical Axe shaft-walking stick
Piolet Rammasse	35-50° Moderate	Horixontal Axe shaft - brace
Piolet Ancre	45-60° + Steep	Vertical Axe -hooking pick

The ankle is required to be very flexible and because of the limited range of flexion forwards and upwards on the steeper slopes the climber always faces outwards. This necessitates a crab like movement in a diagonal ascent with the moving leg crossing high over the stationary leg with the danger of crampon snagging. Turning is accomplished most easily by pivoting on the axe in the Ramasse position (cross body brace) or hanging from the Ancre position (hooked pick placement).

Descending
It is possible to descend and ascend on moderately steep slopes by walking straight up and down facing out from the slope. This requires practice on hard ice. In the descent the axe can be picked into the ice below and ahead of the climber. The axe hand is slid down the shaft which is used as a bannister or hand rail as the climber descends. On steeper terrain the axe will be in the hooking position, *piolet ancre,* with body twisted sideways. The application of French techniques should be limited to the moderate slopes and as

DESCENDING

EN CANARD
DUCK WALK

LEFT HAND SLIDES DOWN
AXE SHAFT FOR SUPPORT

PIOLET RAMPE

RESTING

RESTING
FRONT POINTS
KNEES ON ICE

RESTING - SITTING ON RIGHT FOOT
FLAT FOOTED
PIED ASSIS

soon as the climber feels awkward he should adopt the front point position. On vertical ice it is better to place anchors and abseil.

Crampon Exercises
There are a number of useful crampon exercises which help develop skill:

1. TURNING PRACTICE - On 45° ice, practice moving from front pointing facing in to flat footed facing out by turning around first in one direction and then in the other direction. Gradually progress to steeper and steeper ice eventually using the ice axe hooked in *piolet ancre* for security.

2. GIANT STEPS - Take great big steps on easy angled ice and experience the difficulty of centering - lunging of the body weight occurs. Shorten your steps and consciously move body weight from over one foot to over the other. Check by lifting unweighted foot up and straight out from ice.

3. ALTERNATE HOPPING - On easy angled ice practice lifting one leg in the air and hopping from one foot to the other gradually increasing the size of the step.

Resting Positions
The conservation of energy and the ability to rest are extremely important in ice climbing. Resting positions are when the legs are straight and the joints locked with the body weight being supported by the bones, not the muscles or when the legs are in full squat position. Thus the opposite limits of movement, full extension and full flexion, are resting positions and any unsupported position in between puts tension on the different muscle groups.

a. FRONT POINT RESTING, MODERATE ICE - Face the ice, front pointing one leg extended and one leg in the full squat, place both knees against the ice slope and sit on heel of squatted leg. Alternate this position by changing legs over.

b. *PIED ASSIS* - When walking sideways on 45° ice with French technique squat on the outside leg bringing the heel up under the right buttock with the toes pointing down and out. Alternate this position switching legs.

c. AMERICAN TECHNIQUE, *PIED À TROIS* - is a combination of the front point and the flat footed technique with one foot flat and the other foot front pointing. This can be used on steep ice with the axe in the hooked position. It has the advantage of reducing the strain on the leg muscles by alternating the legs and is a useful out position when front pointing. The flat foot is at 3 o'clock to the front point foot and the ankle joint rolled outwards.

d. RESTING EXTENDED X POSITION - Another resting position front pointing is to be fully extended hanging from the hooked axes, arms straight, wrists cocked in the wrist loops *'piolet traction'*, legs straight and bowed with crampon heels dropped. Relax and breath deeply and slowly letting the bone structure take the body weight.

German Technique
The German technique or *pied en avant* is where the front points only are used to climb the ice. This technique is best examined on very steep or vertical ice where it is taken to its logical limit. The foot is placed rather than kicked hard into the ice as a sharp blow will result in a simultaneous rebound effect and may also shatter the ice if it is at all brittle. It is important to place the boot square on the ice so that both points have an equal purchase. The movement must be positive and firm with the climber transferring the complete body weight alternately from one foot to the other. The resolution of forces ensures that the body weight pushes the crampon points further into the ice. Any hesitation or temerity reduces the effectiveness of the purchase. The sole of the foot must be kept horizontal to maintain the correct angle of penetration of the crampon points. If the heel is too low the crampon points penetrate at the wrong angle and slide out when weight is applied. If the heel is raised when placing the crampon the toe of the boot hits the surface of the ice first and prevents full penetration of the front points. Once the foot has been correctly placed it is important not to have any up and down movement as this will fracture the ice and destroy the placement. The angle of placement of the foot is always relative to the slope angle and on the easier-angled slopes the heel may appear slightly raised. It is normal technique to drop the heel slightly on easy-angled slopes so that more weight is put on the front two downward pointing crampon points.

The great problem which retarded the utilisation of front pointing technique on steep ice was the necessity for some form of handhold. This was partially solved by using ice daggers which were thrust or hammered into the ice and used as handholds. This was sufficient on short steep sections but proved to be difficult to apply to longer ice

FRONT POINT REPLACEMENT

1/HEEL TOO HIGH
TOE PREVENTS PENETRATION
OF FRONT POINTS

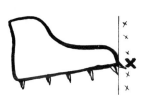

2/HEEL TOO LOW
FRONT POINTS
AT THE WRONG ANGLE.
IF BOOT IS RAISED THE ICE
AT X WILL SHATTER

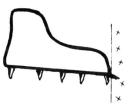

3/BOOT IN CORRECT POSITION
GOOD PLACEMENT

pitches. The solution came from the development of the ice axe and hammer with curved pick which hooked and held in ice. The axe or hammer shaft provided the necessary handhold. The dagger and the hammer were thus combined as a single unit which provided the extra purchase necessary to climb long steep ice pitches. This type of climbing, front pointing and hooking on vertical ice, is strenuous and the climber needs practice to acquire strength and confidence.

The curved axe or hooking technique *piolet traction* should only be used in conjunction with front point techniques on very steep ice, its use on easy-angled ice only encourages incorrect body position and poor technique. The sequence of practice to follow in developing good front point technique, *which is the essential basis of steep ice climbing,* is as follows:

1. Front pointing without axes on short steep sections to develop correct upright body position and good balance.

2. Front pointing on steeper sections using hands on natural ice holds, gaps between the ice and rock. Climbing the ice with rock technique where it is applicable - lay backing, bridging, jamming, mantel-shelfing and chimneying. The French technique, *pied a plat,* will be useful here in conjunction with the above methods of climbing.

3. The use of axes/ hammers on longer, steeper ice with screws as runners. The axes/hammers are only introduced after a considerable amount of front point practice to ensure that the correct body position is attained.

CHAPTER 3
USING THE AXE

Axe Positions
1. *Walking Position*
When walking on the flat, or gentle slopes the axe may be carried gun fashion with the shaft under the arm, the spike forward, and the pick curving up the line of the shoulder blade. This is comfortable and easily accessible but does not leave the hands free. The axe may be carried in the hand like a walking stick with the pick held either pointing forwards or backwards. The Alpine guides generally hold the pick forward to avoid impaling themselves if they trip or stumble. When walking on slopes where there is a possibility of a slip or fall the axe should be carried pick pointing backwards. In this position the axe is ready to be brought up and into the self-arrest position without further adjustment. It is possible that valuable time will be lost in turning the axe from the pick forward position to the pick backward position in the event of a slip. The exception to this rule may be on a slope of soft snow where the adze rather than the pick may be more successful in arresting a fall.

N.B.   The axe should not be carried with the shaft in the horizontal position as there is a danger of injuring the person in front or behind depending on which way the spike is pointing.

2. *Support Position - Piolet Canne*
When ascending, traversing or descending steep snow slopes the axe is used as a third leg, hand over the head and the shaft thrust into the snow on the uphill side for support. The movement should be in a set sequence - Axe in, right leg, left leg, Axe out, Axe in, so that there are always two points of contact to the slope in the event of a slip. This is known as the security pause and should always be used when kicking steps up a slope.

3. *Brace Position - Piolet Ramasse*
This is used on moderate slopes 35-50° for extra security - the axe is held horizontally across the front of the body with the hand nearest the slope pressing down on the ferrule and shaft and the other hand pulling up on the adze head. The spike is firmly embedded in the snow. This method is used in conjunction with conventional step

kicking or with the French method of cramponing *'pied a plat'*. It requires a great deal of practice and confidence, especially when cramponing on ice but once the skill is acquired a great deal of weight is taken off the legs, thus easing the strain on the ankles. The axe position is similar in some respects to the shaft or glissade brake and it is quite easy to turn the body out from the slope to attain this position.

4. Anchor Position - Piolet Ancre

The anchor position is used on steeper slopes, 45-60 + °, than the Brace position. The pick is firmly planted in the snow, with the uphill hand held over the top of the axe for extra security and the shaft held at ferrule or above by the other hand. In crusted snow it may be more effective to reverse the pick and use the adze as the holding surface. This method of using the axe has the advantage that it is ready in the braking position and can easily be moved down to the shoulder for use. It is a good method of ascending a slope used in conjunction with step kicking or following a line of existing steps. On ice the pick will only penetrate a short distance and is generally used with the French method of cramponing *'pied a plat'* or the American *'pied a trois'*.

5. Hooking Position - Piolet Traction - Two Axe or Axe Hammer Technique

This is the basic method of climbing steep ice and is used in conjunction with the front point technique of cramponing. Two axes or ice hammers are required, one in each hand, which are inserted into the ice at full stretch above the climber's head. The climber then crampons up pulling on both his arms until his shoulder is level with the lower part of the axe shaft. First one axe is extracted and re-inserted securely above the climber's head. Hanging from this axe the climber extracts the lower axe and re-inserts alongside the upper axe. He then crampons up until the axes are at shoulder level and repeats the sequence. On short bulges it is possible to crampon up and mantelshelf over the inserted axe/hammer to gain the easier angled ground above.

This is a strenuous method of climbing and requires training and progressive practice. The strain on the hands and forearms can be reduced by using short wrist loops fastened to the shaft above the hand grip. Another method which is very effective is a short wrist sling fastened to the head of the axe and wound around the shaft and looped around the wrist to give extra support.

AXE POSITIONS FRENCH TECHNIQUE

BRACE POSITION
PIOLET RAMASSE

ANCHOR POSITION
PIOLET ANCRE

AXE POSITION FRONT POINTING

PIOLET TRACTION.
1/FRONT POINTING
PICKS HOOKING INTO ICE

2/FRONT POINTING
DAGGERING POSITION
PIOLET ANCRE

SINGLE AXE TECHNIQUE
ANCHOR POSITION
PIOLET ANCRE

HAND POSITIONS FOR DAGGER TECHNIQUE

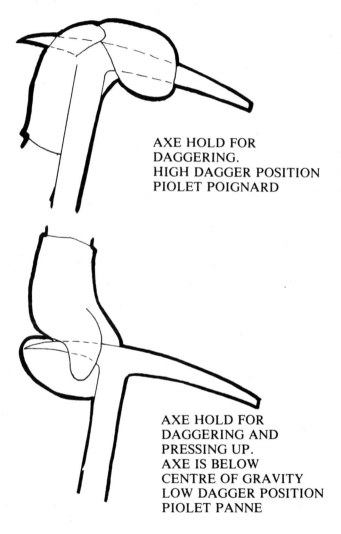

AXE HOLD FOR
DAGGERING.
HIGH DAGGER POSITION
PIOLET POIGNARD

AXE HOLD FOR
DAGGERING AND
PRESSING UP.
AXE IS BELOW
CENTRE OF GRAVITY
LOW DAGGER POSITION
PIOLET PANNE

On vertical ice it is better to use an ice axe and an ice hammer as they give a very secure purchase. When the surface ice is rotten then the longer pick of an ice axe allows penetration to good ice underneath and the two axes should be used. On hollow ice it is probably better to revert to step cutting as jug holds can easily be made by cutting through the surface ice to form a pocket hole. The curved pick technique will not hold on hollow or very thin ice as there is insufficient ice for the pick to secure a firm purchase. On thin ice small incut niches should be cut for the fingers to give support in balance climbing.

6. Dagger Position - Piolet Panne/Piolet Poignard
The dagger position is used with two axes or an axe and a hammer axe and the front point crampon technique on steep slopes of snow and ice. The hands are held either above or below the heads of the axes depending upon the slope angle and the condition of the snow and ice. When the hands are above the axe head the pick is inserted at waist level, *piolet panne*. The main body weight is thus pressing the pick into the slope and some of the strain can be taken off the legs by the arms. On the steeper slopes this position becomes unstable as the upper body and the centre of gravity is pushed away from the slope. On very steep hard snow the hand position will be reversed and the pick inserted at head level, *piolet poignard*. If the snow is soft and the shaft of the axe is thrust into the snow to act as a dagger - this is the 'shaft dagger' position described below. On ice over 60° the dagger position must be replaced by the position which allows greater force to be applied and consequently gives better pick penetration.

7. Support Position - Piolet Rampe
This support position may at first seem ungainly but it does give a surprising amount of stability when descending. The climber descends feet flat on the ice slope facing out the way, the axe is picked into the ice downslope and the hand slid along the shaft which is used as a bannister rail for support. Having descended a few steps the climber stops, extracts the axe, re-inserts it downslope and repeats the manoeuvre.

8. Shaft Dagger Position
The shaft dagger position is used on very steep snow slopes and where the snow is not firm enough to support the pick of the axe. The shaft is held like a dagger in the hand, thrust into the snow, and used as a handhold. It is important to remember to grip the shaft

where it meets the surface of the snow to avoid any leverage. This method is very effective using two axes or an axe and a northwall hammer.

9. Mantelshelfing

In gullies with very steep exits or in trenches cut through cornices it is often necessary to use the axe shaft hammered into the snow as the only means of obtaining a secure hold. This is especially so in softer snow which will not support the climber's weight in steps. this is one of the rare instances when a long axe is more valuable. The climber places the axe shaft down at about 60 - 70° from the snow surface and mantelshelfs up on the axe head to place a second axe if necesary to reach the exit. There are occasions when two or more axes are required to secure an exit in this way. The leader can leapfrog the axes if necessary, using his second's ice axe which can then be lowered to him on the rope or slide down on a karabiner if there are no runners obstructing the rope.

Axe Positions For Front Pointing

Piolet Panne	- low dagger	30-65°	Moderate
Piolet Poingnard	- high dagger	45-65° +	Steep

These are more useful on snow than on ice.

Piolet Ancre	Steep
Piolet Traction	Very Steep Hooking

Glissading

Glissading is an extremely dangerous method of descending a slope and should only be used on slopes with a suitable snow surface and safe runout. Any person who glissades must be competent at ice axe braking. The glissade can be controlled by the axe using the glissade brake and by the climber edging with his feet as in skiing. The body is turned so one is descending in a steep diagonal and the speed is controlled by side slipping and edging. This is achieved by moving the sole of the feet parallel to the slope and then turning them into the horizontal plane so that the edge of the sole acts as a brake and in some instances piles the snow up underneath as a cushion. This cannot be practised on hard snow which should be descended using crampons facing in the usual way. The sitting glissade is easier than the standing glissade and is more stable but it is rather sloppy

GLISSADING

STANDING GLISSADE

technique. It is probably better to persevere and practice the standing glissade as it makes one more aware of the importance of balance which plays a vital part in snow and ice technique.

Abseiling on Snow and Ice

Using modern techniques and equipment which permit rapid movement up and down ice, the necessity to abseil should only arise on very steep terrain, across bergschrunds and on mixed climbs. the technique is the same as that used on rock except that crampons should always be worn on hard névé and ice. On mixed ground care should be taken not to snag crampon points, and large bounding abseils should be avoided for the same reason. Care should also be taken not to tread on the abseil rope with crampons. All climbing equipment, especially ice axes and hammer slings, should be kept out of the way of the abseil rope, especially if a descendeur is being used. The abseil position is leaning well back with the feet braced apart for stability.

Recovering an Ice Screw on a Rappel

An interesting method of recovering a Salewa tubular ice screw after it has been used for a rappel was demonstrated to me by the French guide Walter Cecchinal. The screw is inserted part way with the eye hole pointing upwards. A piece of ½" tape or nylon line is tied to the eye hole and wound around the shaft of the screw in the right direction to extract the screw. This is then attached to a prusik sling fastened to the rappel rope. When the rope is pulled the screw is rotated and extracted. It is important to have sufficient turns around

RECOVERING ICE SCREW ON A RAPPEL

NYLON CORD WOUND AROUND SHAFT IN
RIGHT DIRECTION TO
EXTRACT SCREW

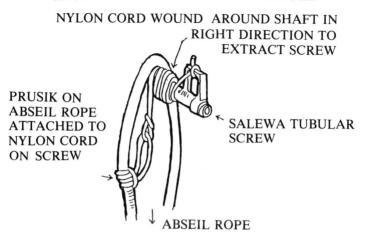

PRUSIK ON
ABSEIL ROPE
ATTACHED TO
NYLON CORD
ON SCREW

SALEWA TUBULAR
SCREW

ABSEIL ROPE

RECOVERING AN ICE AXE ON A RAPPEL

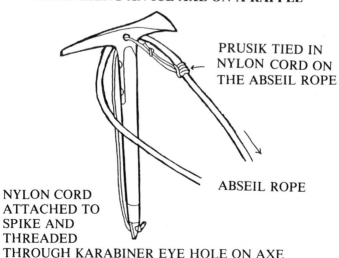

PRUSIK TIED IN
NYLON CORD ON
THE ABSEIL ROPE

ABSEIL ROPE

NYLON CORD
ATTACHED TO
SPIKE AND
THREADED
THROUGH KARABINER EYE HOLE ON AXE

the screw to ensure its complete extraction. This will vary according to the length of the ice screw.

Recovering an Ice Axe on a Rappel
A similar method can be used to retrieve an ice axe after it has been used to reinforce a snow mushroom used as an abseil point. A nylon line is attached to the spike of the axe (some axes have a hole for this purpose) run up the shaft and threaded through the karabiner eye hole at the head of the axe. The line is attached one side of the rappel rope with a prusik sling. When the rope is pulled the axe is extracted by the sling. Care should be taken not to be hit by the falling axe during the retrieval operation.

Moving Together on Snow and Ice
The question of moving together on snow and ice is one which raises many questions of safety. There is little justification in my mind for climbers of equal ability moving roped together on a pure ice climb. They would be much safer climbing unroped. Safety in this situation lies in the person's personal ability and technique. If the situation is serious they could of course climb in the conventional way and belay at the end of each pitch. The decision on a climb is theirs - one of simply climbing roped in the conventional manner or unroped. The exception in this case may be the compromise situation where the two climbers move together, the leader placing running belays at frequent intervals, and the second removing them. This can only be used over short distances as the gear accumulates with the second man and has to be changed over. Another compromise method, which has been used for three people climbing together, is to have the first and third man on the rope and the middle man sliding on a karabiner clipped on the climbing rope. The first man climbs a rope length and belays. The middle man climbs the rope safeguarded by a prusik and belays on the leaders anchor point. The leader and the third man climb together using the middle man's belay as a running belay. When the third man reaches the middle man the leader belays and the middle man ascends the rope on a prusik to join the leader and the system is repeated. Additional running belays can be placed by the leader and removed by the middle man. This system is suitable for pure snow and ice climbs. On long ice routes the security of the belays will be an important factor as to whether one climbs roped in the conventional way or unroped. If they are people of different ability the more experienced may feel it better to rope up and move together if time is pressing and the party is on difficult terrain. In my opinion this is a

dangerous practice especially if the run out is of a serious nature, i.e. over a cliff or boulder field. Any decision made ultimately depends upon the *situation* and the *ability* of the persons involved.

When traversing snow covered glaciers it is of course essential to be roped together because of crevasses. One method, for two men moving together, is for each man to tie on 40' from the end leaving 40' between them on a 120' rope. The spare rope would be coiled across their shoulders. The climbers would traverse with the rope taut between them ready to assume the self arrest position in the event their partner fell into a crevasse. In badly crevassed areas the climbers might only move one at a time belaying each other in the conventional way for greater safety. Both men would carry prusik loops already attached to the rope and should be proficient in crevasse rescue methods. In general it is better to have three or more climbers in a party when crossing badly crevassed glaciers.

CHAPTER 4
STEP KICKING AND CUTTING

Kicking Steps

Step kicking is a basis of good movement on snow as it develops rhythm, balance and correct body position. It is a fast and effective way of ascending and traversing slopes of relatively hard snow. The snow is too hard for kicking steps when more than one kick is necessary to gain a purchase. In this case the climber should revert to step cutting which is slower and more laborious. It is essential to have a stiff soled pair of boots with vibram soles in a reasonable condition. When kicking steps with the side of the boots the serrated edge of the vibram sole should be used as saw teeth and the step made with a forward motion of the foot not a pressing down movement. This method of step kicking involves the inside and outside edges of the boot soles of alternate feet. It is important to keep the soles of the feet absolutely horizontal and to use the axe as a third leg with the 'security pause'. The climber should stand upright all the time using his one kicked foothold and his axe purchase for support. He should not lean into the slope. An alternative method on gentle slopes is to hold the ice axe in the pre-braking position.

When kicking steps straight uphill the climber must face square on to the slope and kick his toes in at right angles to the slope face. The axe should be used in the anchor or support position depending on the steepness of the slope. If the condition of the slope changes and necessitates the cutting of steps it is important to kick a large step in the slope in order to have a platform to begin step cutting. It is posssible to be unbalanced from kicked steps by the recoil of cutting the first step. In this instance a second axe or dagger is convenient for additional purchase.

When kicking steps straight downhill the climber proceeds with straight leg and heel into the slope exerting his full weight on each foot alternately. This movement is achieved with a little jump thus adding some momentum to the heel and giving it greater penetration. The ankle is contracted to ensure the heel presents a sharp angle to the slope and forward movement of the body is avoided to prevent the toe dropping and rocking the heel forward in the kicked step. The axe should be held in the prebraking position in instant readiness should the climber slip. The angle of the heel is such that the lip of the kicked step slopes inwards thus giving greater security. Care should be taken using this method if the hardness of the snow varies from place to place. When in doubt cut steps or better still crampon down.

Step Cutting - Snow
When the snow surface is too hard for kicking steps and crampons are not being worn it is necessary to cut steps using the adze of the ice axe. Step cutting is a relatively slow and laborious method of crossing snow slopes but with practice and technique speed can be developed to a reasonable level. The first rule in step cutting is the 'conservation of energy'. This is achieved by avoiding unnecessary cutting, cutting the steps the optimum size, achieving the optimum spacing, and developing a rhythmic movement. The cutting action should be powerful and with the whole arm swinging the axe from a fixed shoulder. No body swing is necessary. Let the axe do the work and concentrate on developing a rhythm. It is important always to remain in the balance position when cutting and not to over stretch as this leads to the assuming of an unstable position which can be tiring and dangerous. When cutting on gentle slopes the axe may be held in the hand nearest the slope. On steep slopes it is more convenient to cut using the outside arm. If the slope is very steep handholds may have to be cut for the inside hand to give additional security.

Types of Steps
1. *Slash Step*
    The slash step is the most economical and fastest way of cutting but it can only be used on snow. The step is cut with one glancing blow of the axe which cuts out a 'slash' five or six inches long in the snow surface sufficient for the edge of the boot. It is important to attain the correct position of cutting; the adze cutting in a vertical plane across the fall line of the slope. The angle of penetration must not be too steep or the adze will stick in the snow and it must not be so shallow as to glance off or miss the snow surface. Once mastered the slash step is by far the fastest method of cutting and can be used in diagonal ascents and descents of slopes.

2. *Side Step*
    The side step is long enough and wide enough to accommodate the whole boot comfortably. The cutting position is the same as for the slash step but the angle of penetration is steeper. The first blow is not too hard otherwise the axe could become

DIAGRAM OF STEP CUTTING
ON SNOW CRUST

1/CUT HORIZONTAL SLIT

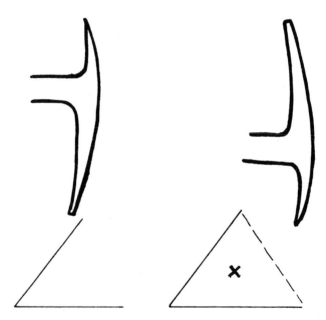

2/CUT DIAGONAL SLIT   3/CHOP OUT SECTION X
WITH THE ADZE

STEP CUTTING

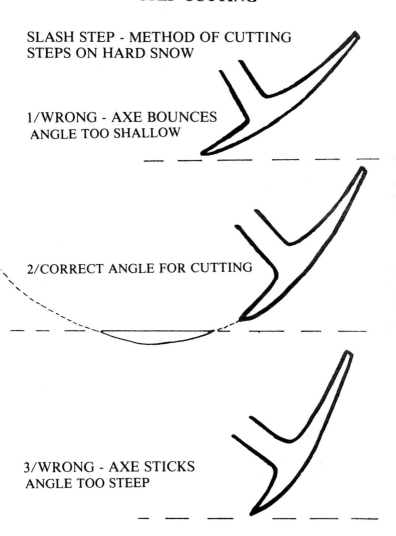

SLASH STEP - METHOD OF CUTTING
STEPS ON HARD SNOW

1/WRONG - AXE BOUNCES
ANGLE TOO SHALLOW

2/CORRECT ANGLE FOR CUTTING

3/WRONG - AXE STICKS
ANGLE TOO STEEP

embedded firmly in the snow and cause difficulty in extraction. A gentle nick is normally sufficient to start and the cut section can be flicked away as the axe is withdrawn for the second blow. The second and third cuts are made into the existing nick thus enlarging it to a step. The step should slope sharply inwards to give greater security. There is no need to clear the debris out of the step completely by scraping as this costs time and energy and will in any case be trodden down by the feet. Only three blows are normally necessary to make a reasonable side step on hard snow.

3. *Slab Cut*
    Under certain conditions when the snow is found to be slabby it may be difficult to cut firm steps in the ways outlined above. In this case the slab cut should be used. First a slit is made with the pick sloped at an angle of 45 degrees then another slit is made horizontally to form a V pointing towards the climber. The axe is then turned and the centre of the V cut out with the adze leaving a triangular step with a flat base. This step is very effective in soft wind slab snow conditions.

4. *The Pigeon Hole Step*
    The pigeon hole step is used for direct ascent on steep snow and is easily cut with two or three blows of the adze. It is important to slope the step well down so that there is a good jug hold for the hand.

Step Cutting - Ice
All step cutting on ice is extremely strenuous and tiring and the rules of energy conservation apply to an even greater extent than they do on snow.

Cutting is hard work and requires physical strength and endurance if it is to be done for long periods. Always look for the natural steps in ice which can be enlarged by a few axe blows and remember that as a general rule the whiter the ice the easier it is to cut. In Scottish and Alpine ice there are often edges between the ice and the rock which can be used as holds. Ice bulges are often followed by softer snow-ice and jug holds can easily be cut at the junction of the hard and the soft ice.

Side Step
Whenever possible cut on ice with the adze of the ice axe in the same

PIGEON HOLE STEPS ON ICE

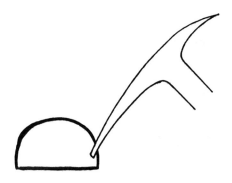

1/ IN HARD ICE
INITIAL CUTTING WITH THE PICK

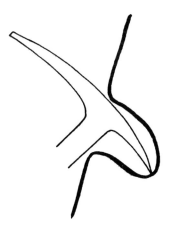

2/SHAPE AND FINISH WITH THE ADZE

way as on snow. The adze should be kept sharp for this purpose and it may be an advantage to carry a file. Sometimes the ice may be very hard and the pick of the ice axe has to be used. In this instance cut a line of incisions down into the ice and then cut along the same line horizontally. Shape and clear the step with the adze. When cutting across ice with no crampons make sure the base of the step slopes inwards and is large enough to give adequate support to the foot.

Pigeon Hole Steps on Ice
The traditional method of climbing steep ice is to cut a ladder of holds or jug handles taking occasional rests on ice screws or ice pitons. The steps which are used both as foot holds and hand holds are cut with the adze and incut at the back using the pick. A pronounced lip is fashioned so that the climber can hold himself on to the ice whilst he is cutting the next step. Various methods may be used to assist this difficult manoeuvre - shaping a ball on the base of the step to give a good grip or fashioning the step a suitable size for jamming the hand in to give additional security. Whatever method is used it is strenuous, laborious and time consuming. Occasionally one finds hollow ice in the Scottish gullies and jug holds can easily be cut. However, the ice may be unsafe and will not hold ice screws.

Ice Nicks/Finger Holds
It is not always necessary to cut large steps in ice. A small nick as an incut finger hold can be fashioned with one or two blows of the adze. This will provide sufficient purchase for a crampon point in brittle ice or for a finger hold for balance climbing. On ice less than one inch thick this technique is often the only possible means of ascent as there is insufficient ice for using the curved hammer techniques safely.

Step Patterns
There are two basic step patterns which can be used in conjunction with the side step, the single and the double. The most convenient method of ascending and descending snow is by a diagonal line as it is easier to cut steps slightly ahead. The single diagonal line of steps is quicker to cut as less steps are needed but it requires greater care in stepping through from one step to the other. The double diagonal requires more time but is possibly safer to use especially if the steps are to be descended later, and provides a stable cutting platform.

It may be safer, especially in descent, not to step through ie. cross one leg past the other to reach the next step, but to constantly

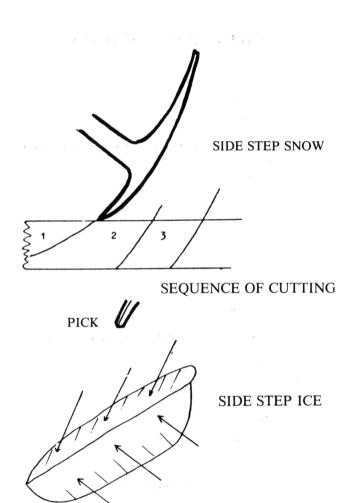

SIDE STEP SNOW

SEQUENCE OF CUTTING

PICK

SIDE STEP ICE

PICK

STEP CUTTING PATTERNS

1/STEEP DIAGONALS SINGLE

2/ STEEP DIAGONALS DOUBLE

3/PIGEON HOLE STEPS

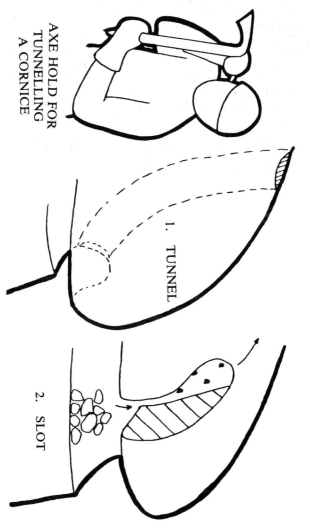

SURMOUNTING A CORNICE

AXE HOLD FOR
TUNNELLING
A CORNICE

1. TUNNEL

2. SLOT

advance the leading foot keeping the trailing foot in the step behind. When the stepping through method is used the rear knee can be locked into the back of the front leg to give a more stable position for cutting. When cutting straight downhill a longer axe may be useful although a short axe can be used by bending at the knee so reaching lower. The steps should have a pronounced lip so they can be used as handholds for the upper hand for additional security. On very steep ground one must always step down with the lower leg first and not step through. It is better on steep ground to descend on a rope and cut back up an ascent line of steps for the descending party.

Step cutting straight up steep snow and ice uses a regular pattern of pigeon hole steps spaced at similar intervals to the rungs of a ladder. It is important to cut well ahead using this pattern and never climb up into the top steps, always have a handhold above you for security.

CHAPTER 5:
ICE AXE SELF-ARREST TECHNIQUES

The ability to stop an involuntary slide or fall on snow is certainly one of the most important skills to be acquired in winter mountaineering. It is not a skill which is acquired easily but requires progressive practice and training. The purpose of this chapter is to examine existing methods of braking and to suggest a system of progressive practice which can be followed to improve a person's personal ability to ice axe brake.

A method of braking advocated by Winthrop Young in *Mountain Craft,* which has been reproduced in several text books, is the two handed technique. The ice axe shaft is tucked under the arm head uppermost and both hands are clasped firmly over the axe head driving the pick into the snow surface. This method has the disadvantage of the shaft projecting up in the air and if any rotation of the climber occurred the axe shaft could dig into the ground and be levered from his grasp. The position is also awkward to adopt when moving across ground where there is a possibility of a slip. Another method which is sometimes seen is with axe held head uppermost parallel with the chest on one side of the body, with one hand over the head and one around the shaft at waist level. It is not possible to exert the body weight on the axe in this position and the climber has to rely on his arm strength in order to apply the brake. This method must also therefore be regarded as unsatisfactory.

A method of ice axe braking used by some Scottish climbers is the thigh brake. In this method the climber lies on his side, feet first on the slope with the lower leg bent and his thigh lying across the fall line of the slope. The axe shaft is placed across the thigh which acts as a fulcrum for the pick to be levered into the slope. One hand is gripping the axe head and the other is holding the shaft below the thigh. The body leans well into the slope and the forearm of the hand holding the axe must be directly above and in line with the ice axe shaft. In this way the body weight is well over the axe head and the degree of pick insertion can easily be controlled. The outside leg is used as a counter weight and is kept pointing straight down hill for stability. The side of the foot may be used as an additional brake and control. It is important not to use the heel as the leg may be jarred by the sudden impact of hitting a rock. This method has the advantages that the climber can see where he is falling; he has good control of

METHODS OF ICE AXE BRAKING

DOUBLE HANDED
SHOULDER BRAKE

SHOULDER BRAKE
ON ONE SIDE

THIGH BRAKE

the depth of the pick; and the greater part of his body weight is above braking point. However, on very steep slopes the high proportion of weight above the braking point may cause rotation of the body and there may be difficulty in assuming and maintaining the self-arrest position. The operation of this method when the climber is wearing crampons may also be difficult as the lower stabilising leg will have to be lifted off the slope to prevent cartwheeling. The adoption and practice of a particular method really depends on one's own personal experience. People who have acquired an effective method of braking over the years should have no necessity to change unless they believe the new method has advantages over the one they practice.

The ice axe shoulder brake is a method which has been used for many years and has proved its worth on many occasions. In this method the axe shaft is held diagonally across the chest, head uppermost, with one hand firmly clasped over the adze and the other over the ferrule and spike. On axes longer than 55cms. the spike and ferrule cannot be covered and consequently must project with some danger of catching below the lower hand. This alone is a strong argument against the longer general mountaineering ice axes. In training sessions many students have found braking with a reasonably short axe far easier than braking with a long axe. Both elbows are tucked well into the sides of the body and the body is hunched over the top adze hand with as much weight as possible over the axe head. The lower hand has a firm control over the shaft to prevent it catching and levering the axe head from the upper hand.

In the event of a fall the person adopts the *braking position* before attempting to brake. This may appear obvious but a common mistake with beginners is to insert the pick and assume the braking position at the same time. The end result is normally a lost ice axe which can be torn from your hands, especially if inserted too hard and too hastily. Speed as well as control is important as the longer the delay in applying the brake the greater the speed of descent. Assuming the climber is sliding feet first down the slope — this is the usual start position for self-arrest practice — his first step is to get into the braking position. He then initiates full body rotation towards the side on which he is holding the ice axe pick by throwing his opposite leg across. Using his elbow as a guide the pick is gradually inserted and full body weight brought to bear on the axe head. In some conditions the climber will stop with the body half turned and the hips turned sideways to the slope. This is the half braking position which some people regard as the full braking

(1) THE BRAKING POSITION

(2) THE HALF BRAKING POSITION

(3) THE FULL BRAKING POSITION

position. To obtain the full braking, rotation is continued until the climber is in the face down position on the slope with his body arched from the toes and the sternum pressing hard against the axe shaft. The lower hand grasping the ferrule holds this shaft end close to the body. The feet can be used to assist braking by digging the toes into the snow. However, if crampons are worn or the slope is very steep it is best to raise the feet to prevent the body cartwheeling backwards. In the maximum braking position the feet are spread apart for stability and to lessen the chance of rotation. It is very important to roll on to the axe head side of the body and not on to the ferrule side, especially if the axe is over 55cms. as there is a danger of the spike entering the snow and the climber losing the axe.

In a training situation the climber would practice this method feet first on his back on the lower part of a concave slope, with no rusksack or crampons on. As ability and confidence increase, longer and faster slides can be attempted high up on the steeper part of the slope. Throughout the training session gloves should be worn to protect the hands and a crash helmet to protect the head. A full waterproof suit, not one with a smooth shiny surface which can be extremely slippery, should be worn and it may be convenient to tuck the cagoule inside the overtrousers. The next stage would be to introduce the technique of turning the body from the head first position on the stomach to the braking position. This is an important technique as in a fall the body tends to adopt the head down position.

A ledge should be cut in the slope for the climber to rest his elbows in and the axe should be held shaft across the face with the pick well to one side. One hand is held over the axe head and one over the ferrule and spike. Care must be taken to keep the adze away from the face to avoid accidental cuts and an adze cover may be fitted if desired. The climber slides downhill a few feet with the pick of the axe clear of the snow. He then inserts the pick well to the side and the body slides past the axe and down into the braking position. This requires several practices and care must be taken to tuck the elbows in as quickly as possible. This practice should be progressive like the first, with steeper slopes and faster slides attempted. The progressive build up of speed is very important as the ability and confidence to brake at speed in the practice situation requires repeated effort. No training session is really effective unless held on hard neve, as soft snow even on steeper slopes gives a false sense of security in braking. In the poorer snow conditions the practice sequence can, however, be taught for future use.

Once the person has mastered the head first stomach descent the next stage is head first on the back. This may initially cause some trepidation with students and the practice should in these instances be controlled manually by the instructor. Again the ledge is utilised with the climber resting his head and shoulders on the edge. The axe is held diagonally across the body with pick inserted out to one side by the climber's thigh. One hand is held over the axe head and the other firmly grasping the shaft. Once the pick is inserted the body pivots down and into the braking postion. As with the previous exercise, the movement requires practice — the legs must be allowed to sweep through so that the braking position can be adopted as quickly as possible. Once the movement is mastered progressive practice can be introduced.

The final stage in the braking practice is the introduction of methods to control rotation. These practices involve the climber in a degree of disorientation which can be dangerous, especially with the sharp points of the ice axe close to the body. Care must be taken and the adze and spike covered with a protective guard. The first step is to perform a single forward roll with the axe held horizontally across the body and the adze held away from the face. Manual control can be used here by the instructor who can also cover the adze head with his hand during the rotation. The student counters the rotation by opening out the body, spreading out the arms and legs but keeping a firm grasp of the axe. The exercise can be repeated with progression to double rolls. The shoulder roll can also be introduced at this stage, where the student rotates diagonally across the slope on his shoulder. The backward roll should not be used as this can lead to complete disorientation and puncture injuries.

The complete training sequence may take several hours on a good training slope and with average students a reasonable degree of proficiency may be attained. However, it must be stressed that repeated practices are necessary in order to maintain the skill. Snow and ice conditions can vary enormously with breakable crust on hard base, wet snow on hard base, powder snow on hard base, soft slab, hard slab, etc., and it will obviously pay to practice on the different snow types. It is important to realise that good climbing conditions, i.e. hard neve and ice, are also optimum conditions for fast sliding and a high degree of skill is required to self arrest on even gentle slopes under these conditions. Ice axe braking on ice is really not a practical proposition and ice patches as well as boulders are often the cause of a climber losing his axe whilst trying to arrest a fall.

ATTAINING THE BRAKING POSITION
FROM THE HEAD FIRST STOMACH POSITION

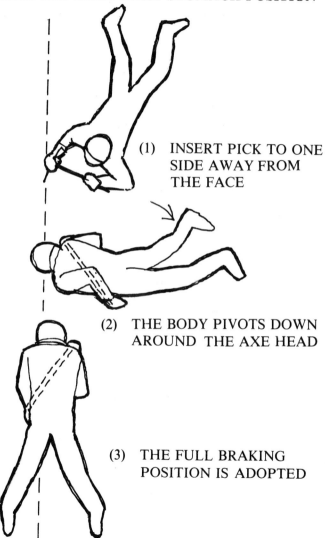

(1) INSERT PICK TO ONE SIDE AWAY FROM THE FACE

(2) THE BODY PIVOTS DOWN AROUND THE AXE HEAD

(3) THE FULL BRAKING POSITION IS ADOPTED

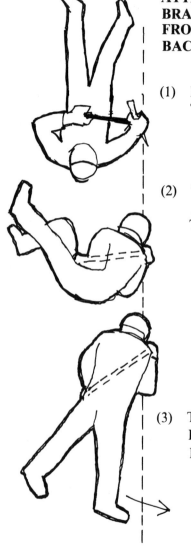

ATTAINING THE BRAKING POSITION FROM THE HEAD FIRST BACK POSITION

(1) INSERT THE PICK TO ONE SIDE

(2) THE BODY PIVOTS AROUND THE AXE HEAD

(3) THE FULL BRAKING POSITION IS ADOPTED

All practice sessions mentioned so far have been without rucksack or crampons and it is advisable that some training take place wearing these accoutrements. The degree and amount of practice under these conditions is a personal decision as braking practice in crampons is a dangerous undertaking and may in some cases cause more accidents than it would save.

The question of whether or not the ice axe should be attached to the climber is a debatable one. Any method used such as the sliding wrist loop, the short shaft sling or the long sling, has the inherent danger that the axe will flail around and injure the climber if he loses grip of it during a fall. It may be the case that more injuries are sustained from the axe than from the fall. Certainly during ice axe braking sessions it is advisable not to have the axe attached to the person. Training sessions should be designed to develop a close affinity between the climber and his axe — it should be regarded as a natural extension of himself.

The effectiveness of different types of axes for self-arrest may vary according to the characteristics of the pick. The curved pick ice axes have a tendency to bite in, causing an upward rotation of the shaft which needs to be firmly controlled. Any axe with a very thin or very short pick may also tend to be less effective as a brake.

Any peculiarities or shortcoming of your own particular axe will become evident during self-arrest training sessions and it may just be a matter of familiarisation.

There is another method of braking using the shaft of the ice axe which is used in soft snow and in controlling a glissade. This shaft or glissade brake can be used in the standing or the sitting position. The axe is held shaft down by the side with the nearside hand on the shaft pushing down and acting as a fulcrum and the other hand holding and pulling back on the axe head. The shaft is thus forced into the snow to act as a brake. It is necessary to keep the axe close to the side for greater control and stability. Glissading is the cause of many accidents as people often lose control and it should only be attempted on easy slopes with safe runouts and by people very experienced in ice axe braking.

The greatest dangers involved in a slip on ice or snow are the tendency for the body to rotate, also to adopt the head down position. It is possible with practice to rectify this situation and bring oneself into a position where it is possible to self-arrest. However, the acquisition of this skill requires practice under safe control

CONTROLLING ROTATION

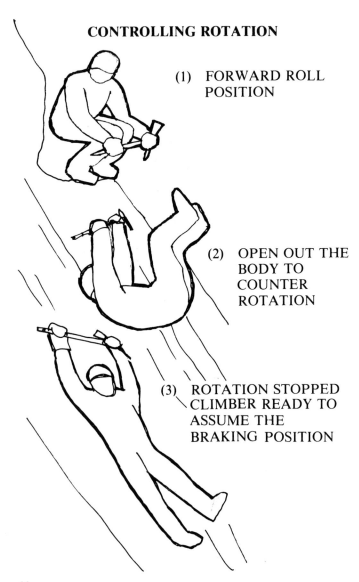

(1) FORWARD ROLL POSITION

(2) OPEN OUT THE BODY TO COUNTER ROTATION

(3) ROTATION STOPPED CLIMBER READY TO ASSUME THE BRAKING POSITION

conditions and with, in some cases, experienced supervision and instruction. Always remember it is not the mere possession of an ice axe which is your safety insurance on the hill in winter, it is the wherewithal to use it!

CHAPTER 6:
SNOW AND ICE ANCHORS AND BELAYING

Whenever possible rock belays should be sought for as they are far superior to any snow or ice belay. However, this is not always possible and other methods have to be employed.

All anchors on snow and ice depend ultimately upon the anchoring material which depends upon age, density, temperature. It is important to be familiar with the different snow and ice conditions (see Appendix) and to use the appropriate equipment.

Ice Bollard
In spite of the advances in ice screw design this is still probably the best belay on ice. A bollard is cut out of a solid boss of ice about 18 inches across and 24 inches long. The trench should be 6 inches deep and cut in at the back to hold the rope in position. Any starring or opaqueness in the centre of the bollard is an indication that it is unsound.

Natural Anchors
Occasionally, natural ice anchors occur - ice pillars, natural ice pinnacles, edges and flakes of ice which can be cut into anchor points with the ice axe.

Snow Anchors
The most effective belay on snow is the deadman. This consists of a flat alloy plate about one foot square with a four foot wire sling attached to its centre. A 'T' shaped slot is cut in the snow slope with care being taken not to disturb the snow on the down slope side. The plate is then inserted at an angle of about 40 degrees to the snow slope. This angle is obtained by placing an ice axe perpendicular to the slope and bisecting the angle between the shaft and the slope with the deadman; cast the deadman plate back a few degrees from this. Attach another sling to the wire sling to give a length of at least 6 feet and pull it tight in the centre slot. Check the depth of the deadman, using the axe to measure the distance from the wire attachment point to the surface of the snow. Cut a stance below the sling and belay in the normal way. Check that the deadman is 'seated' by pulling tight on the belay. Avoid placing the deadman between two snow layers of

SNOW ANCHORS

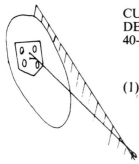

CUT A 'T' SLOT AND INSERT
DEADMAN AT AN ANGLE OF
40-45 DEGREES TO THE SLOPE

(1)   DEADMAN ANCHOR

THE BACK MAY BE REINFORCED
WITH AN ICE AXE OR PADDED
WITH A RUCKSACK

(2)   SNOW MUSHROOM

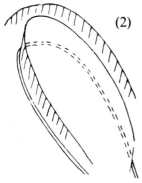

ICE ANCHORS

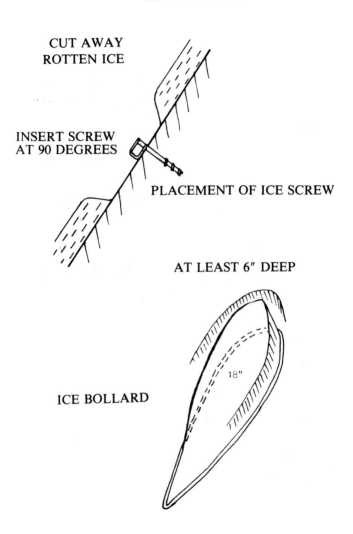

CUT AWAY
ROTTEN ICE

INSERT SCREW
AT 90 DEGREES

PLACEMENT OF ICE SCREW

AT LEAST 6″ DEEP

ICE BOLLARD

18″

DINNER PLATING

STARRING ASSOCIATED WITH OPAQUENESS IN THE ICE

different hardness.

In the absence of a deadman a sling may be clove hitched around the shaft of the ice axe and the axe buried in the horizontal position in a T shaped slot. A shovel, ski, or piece of board may also be used.

There are now deadmen which are bent on the vertical axis to form a snow fluke which supposedly increases the stability and reduces rotation about that axis. The flat plate may also have bent flanges on the vertical edges for the same reason. In some models the cable yoke is fixed at two points on the deadman plate at a set angle as compared with the normal loop form of yoke. The relative merits of these has yet to be determined and it is my opinion that *careful* placement is the greatest insurance for anchor security.

Ice Screws
The modern developments in ice screws have greatly improved security as anchors, however, the crucial factor remains the condition of the ice.

There are three basic types of ice pitons.
i.   The drive-in cut-out old conventional type, which may now be regarded as obsolete.
ii.   The drive-in screw-release piton i.e. Snarg or the Chouinard/ Salewa Warthog.
iii.   The screw-in/Screw release piton i.e. Chouinard tubular or the M.S.R. tubular or the Russian titanium ice screw.

There is no ice screw or piton which is the ideal - they each have their advantages and disadvantages and one must use different screws for different types of ice. The effectiveness of any ice screw ultimately depends upon the strength of the ice. When placing an ice screw, check the ice carefully for thickness and density - colour will be of help in determining good ice. Avoid placing screws vertically on the lip of steps of ice and always place screws at least one metre apart to avoid weakening the ice.

1.   Always cut away rotten ice so that the piton can be placed in the strongest ice available - this may mean cutting away 6″-9″ of ice in some cases.

2.   During placement look carefully for starring-fracturing of the ice which is often followed by dinner plating - detachment of discs of ice around the ice screw. This is particularly true in brittle ice. It often helps to pick a small hole so that the thread on the tubular

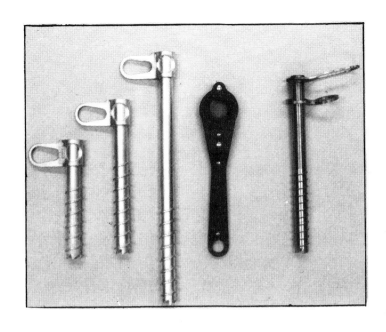

ICE PITONS
Chouinard 11, 17, 28cm. Ice Screws
Chouinard ratchet
Russian Titanium machine
Cut threads

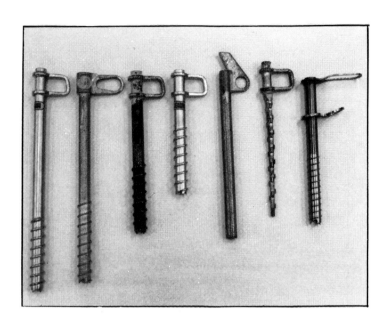

ICE PITONS
Assorted Ice Screws

ICE SCREW PLACEMENT

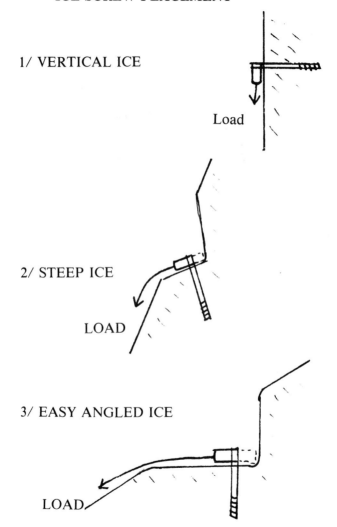

1/ VERTICAL ICE

Load

2/ STEEP ICE

LOAD

3/ EASY ANGLED ICE

LOAD

screws can bite and penetrate more easily. When the temperature is at or below freezing the ice piton will freeze into greater security. Above freezing the pitons will tend to absorb heat and melt out. It is possible to pack snow around the screw to reduce the likelihood of this occurrence, however, this is only a short term remedy.

Ice strength improves with decreasing temperatures. Therefore colder ice is stronger ice although below -10°C ice becomes very brittle and liable to dinner plate where screws are placed. Water ice is surprisingly strong with densities between ·75 and ·88 compared with with glacier ice of ·84 to ·90. The longer the ice screw the greater its holding power so always use long screws for belay anchors.

Tubular Screws
The Chouinard Salewa ice screws are 20mm in diameter and are hollow, making them suitable for brittle ice as it extracts a core of ice as it is screwed in. Examination of the core will reveal clues to the ice quality as will the amount of strength required to place the screw. Once used tubular screws become choked and require cleaning with a Warthog ice piton or thin steel rod. It is possible to melt out the ice by carrying the screw inside a jacket or heating it over a small portable gas stove carried for that purpose. In good ice the tubular screws have been tested up to 2000 kilos but even so, one should always use multiple anchors linked with a self-equalizing belay system. The angle of placement of ice screws is 90° to the ice on vertical ice faces to facilitate rotation of the eye. On easier angled ice, steps can be cut and the screw placed 45° up against the direction of the pull. On low angle ice a step can be cut and the screw placed vertically downwards at the back of the step. The Chouinard/Salewa Ultra tubular screw is available in three lengths 17, 22 and 30cm.

The Warthog is a drive in screw release piton which is useful in soft ice but has less holding power - 1000 kilos - than the tubular ice screws.

The Snarg Ice Piton designed by Lowe Alpine systems is a tubular drive-in ice piton with excellent holding power and minimal dinnerplating. It is threaded for easy screw out removal and has a full length slot to facilitate the removal of the ice core.

Ice Tool Anchors
The new ice climbing hooked and inclined picks can also be used as 'back up' anchors on the main belay. If there are karabiner eye holes on the ferrule/spike the anchor rope can be clovehitched to them or

if umbilical cords are used the tools can be placed with these in tension.

Certain well placed axes have been tested up to 4000 lbsf. which indicates that a directionally loaded axe can provide a good back up anchor. *(ACC Gazette No. 102, Autumn 1983).*

Belaying Techniques on Snow and Ice

The basic types may be divided into DIRECT and INDIRECT and the method of belaying into static and dynamic. The direct belay is where the rope is used directly around the anchor; the indirect belay is where the belayer is anchored and is holding the rope around his body or in a belay device to provide additional security and control of friction. The static belay is one which averts a fall without allowing any rope movement and is really only applicable when a leader is belaying the second man from ABOVE. The dynamic belay requires the rope to slide under friction thereby absorbing some of the energy from the fall and reducing the force on the belayer and on the falling climber. A dynamic belay should always be used when the second man is belaying the leader.

The following methods of belaying can be used on snow and ice:

1. Direct Pick Belay
2. Direct Shaft Belay
3. Ice Piton Foot Brake
4. Ice Axe Foot Brake
5. The Stomper Belay
6. The Conventional Waist Belay - indirect belay
7. Belay Devices

1. The Direct Pick Belay

The direct pick belay is where the live climbing rope runs across the top of the pick when the ice axe is in the anchor position on ice. This is a quick method of belaying but has little to recommend it from the point of view of security apart from speed.

2. The Direct Shaft Belay

The ice axe is thrust down into the snow and the knee securely braced against it to give additional support. The live climbing rope is paid around the head and held in both hands. Again the great advantages of the direct static belay are the speed and relative simplicity with

DIRECT BELAYS ON SNOW AND ICE

ICE AXE SHAFT BELAY (DIRECT)

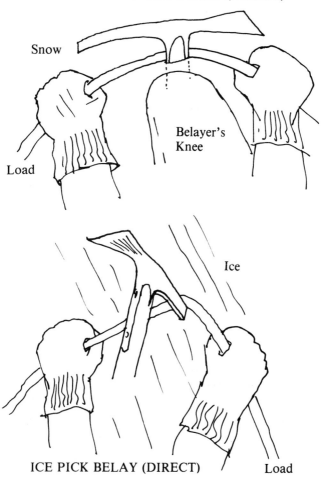

Snow

Belayer's
Knee

Load

Ice

ICE PICK BELAY (DIRECT)

Load

which they can be brought into operation. However, they are not efficient in holding leader falls and their use is best limited to safeguarding seconds climbing directly below the belayer.

3. The Ice Piton Foot Brake (direct/dynamic)

A far better method of belaying on ice is to use the ice piton foot brake. First cut a step in the ice slope and insert an ice peg vertically near the back of the step. Next, two screw gate karabiners are clipped together and one is clipped into the eye of the ice peg. The belay rope is twisted around the back of the bar of the lower karabiner and brought around the uphill foot of the belayer which is placed on top of the piton and first krab. In the event of a fall the rope is allowed to run and is slowly arrested by turning it against the foot with the uphill hand. Properly executed this forms a good method of belaying but it requires practice to perfect.

4. The Ice Foot Brake (direct/dynamic)

This method is similar to the ice piton foot brake in that it is a sliding friction arrest using an inserted ice axe. First the axe is inserted to the head on the uphill side of the belayer who places his foot firmly against the axe head. The rope runs around the outside, i.e. uphill side of the axe shaft across the front of the boot and is held in the downhill hand. The uphill hand holds the axe head firmly and the body weight is pressed onto the uphill knee reinforcing the position of the foot holding the axe in place. In the event of a fall the rope is allowed to run and is gradually arrested by moving it across the instep of the uphill foot. This technique does require considerable practice and at least 30 feet of spare rope to ensure a successful arrest. When this technique is being used it is important not to lead out the full rope length but leave 30 feet available to the belayer in the event of a fall. Obviously the technique is only applicable on falls where no running belays are used. Its main application is when two climbers are moving together across a slope carrying coils. In the event of a fall the stationary climber drops his coils, inserts his axe and operates the foot brake. It is quicker and safer in this instance to carry the rope already around the shaft of the axe where it is held in place by the fingers. In some conditions, i.e. hard snow, it is not possible to insert the axe to the hilt - in this case the uphill knee should be advanced and braced against the axe shaft giving it additional support.

ICE AXE FOOT BRAKE

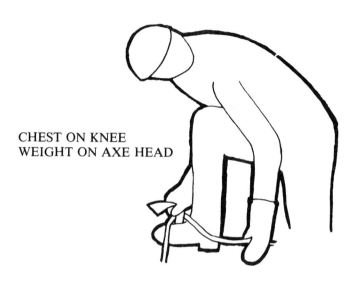

CHEST ON KNEE
WEIGHT ON AXE HEAD

ON VERY HARD SNOW
KNEE BRACES AXE

ICE PITON FOOT BRAKE

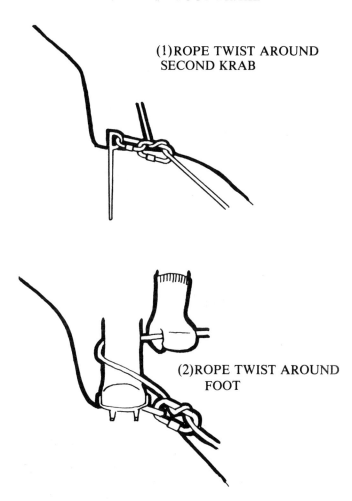

(1) ROPE TWIST AROUND SECOND KRAB

(2) ROPE TWIST AROUND FOOT

STOMPER BELAY

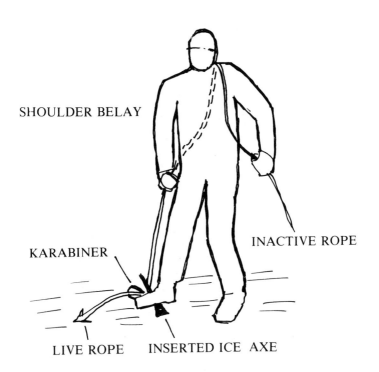

SHOULDER BELAY

KARABINER

INACTIVE ROPE

LIVE ROPE   INSERTED ICE AXE

5. **The Stomper Belay**   (direct/dynamic)
The stomper belay is useful on level glaciers or at the top of routes
above the cornice. An ice screw or ice axe is placed vertically in the
ice or snow and a karabiner attached through the eye hole. The live
climbing rope is clipped up through the karabiner and the belayer
stands on the anchor and adopts a shoulder belay. When the rope is
loaded the full weight of the belayer is pulled down onto the anchor.
It is important not to lean forward when using this belay otherwise
the rope will be pulled over the head and off the shoulder. The body
position should be as follows:

1. Feet apart for stability
2. Knee on load side locked and the foot firmly braced on the ice screw/ice axe
3. Leaning back with straight back
4. Both hands on the rope

6. The Conventional Waist Belay - indirect belay

The indirect belay involves the introduction of the climber into the belay chain between the anchor point and the moving climber.

The waist/hip belay is widely used as the standard indirect dynamic belay with minor technical differences in different places. The belaying rope may run over the top of the anchor rope in which case it is more difficult to arrest an upward pull arising from a leader fall with running belays. It is, however, effective on downward pulls. An alternative is to run the belaying rope under the anchor rope so that an upward fall can more easily be arrested. In this case if no runners are in place or if runner failure occurs the rope is in an extremely difficult position to hold. A possible solution to this dilemma is to clip the belaying rope through a karabiner attached to the waist line thus securing it from a pull in either direction. The position of the belaying hand on the rope may also vary according to the degree of friction required. In the U.K. it is standard practice to have a twist of rope around the belay arm on the inactive side thus ensuring more body/rope contact and consequently more friction. It has a disadvantage, however, in that a full rope length fall may result in the belayer's arm being pulled around and trapped behind his back. This actually happened to a climber and he had to be rescued from this helpless position. The alternative method without a twist provides less friction but removes this danger.

The introduction of a climbing harness into the waist belay system solves some problems and creates others. It is important when using the dynamic waist belay that the rope linking the anchor and the belayer be attached to the back or side of the body. The normal 'tie in' to the end of the rope or to the waist belt can easily be swivelled round to the back for the correct belay attachment position. When a harness with a fixed front attachment point is used a bight of the rope must be taken, tied off and clipped into a back waist loop. This modification is not necessary if a secure running belay is placed close to the belay station. In this instance the climber can belay standing sideways tying into a separate anchor.

METHOD OF ANCHORING WHEN USING A HARNESS WITH A FRONT ATTACHMENT POINT

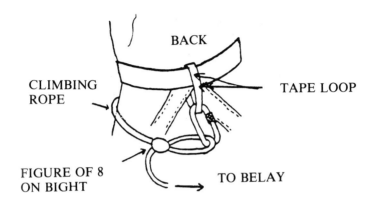

PROS

1. Anchor attachment at rear.
2. Belayer can remove himself from the system by untying front attachment.

CONS

1. Awkward to arrange.
2. Slow.

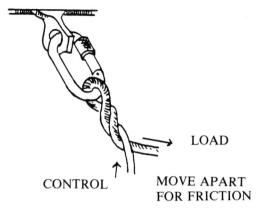

LOAD

CONTROL   MOVE APART
FOR FRICTION

SAXON CROSS

This can be used on rock and ice piton and around the shaft of an ice axe.

1. Cannot be used on a flexible attachment point. i.e. sling or wire chock as the twists will transfer from the rope to the attachment point!
2. Should only be used on anchor points which will withstand multi-directional forces.

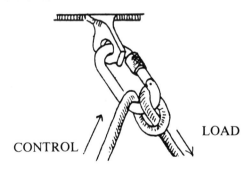

LOAD

CONTROL

ITALIAN OR MUNTER HITCH

1. Not suitable for use on Hawser laid rope.
2. Should only be used on anchor points which will withstand multi-directional forces.
3. Tying off load with prusik sling fastened by a Mariner Knot (releases under load).

7. Belay Devices

It is important that there are many variables to consider when using the waist belay and it is hardly surprising that mechanical belay devices or friction knots have been developed, ie. the sticht plate and the Italian hitch. These may be used on the climbing harness to give an indirect belay.

The advent of mechanical belay devices and belay friction hitches which give a dynamic belay allow the direct belay to be used for belaying the leader. It is important to remember that with the direct belay the load comes directly onto the anchor point and it is consequently subjected to a greater loading than a properly executed indirect belay. When using the direct dynamic belay the belayer should be secured to a separate anchor point unless speed is important and the party is moving together (he may stop occasionally to give his partner a quick direct dynamic belay across a short difficult section). The belay friction hitch used as a direct dynamic belay with the belayer anchored separately has the advantage of effectively separating the belayer from the belay system. In the event of a fall, little strain comes onto the belayer and he is able to tie off and secure the second man and remove himself from the system. (See diagram). In order to tie off the load rope a 5mm or 7mm sling can be attached to it using a prusik knot and the free end can be clipped into a separate anchor point. This can only be released by lifting the load to slacken the knot or by cutting the sling. A solution to this problem is to tie the end of the prusik sling onto the anchor karabiner with a mariner knot (See diagram) which can be released under the load. The direct dynamic belay can be used on snow using the ice axe foot brake and on ice using the ice piton foot brake. Both of these methods require considerable skill and practice to execute effectively and in both cases the belayer is in an unstable position in the event of anchor failure. Probably a better belaying technique is to use a Saxon cross knot on the ice shaft or ice piton, as this eliminates the need of a boot for friction. The belayer faces into the snow slope with one hand braced on the head of the inserted ice axe and the other controlling the rope which normally has a minimum of 3 twists. This 'tripod position' has the advantage of being more stable than the boot axe position.

As a general rule on snow and ice the safest procedure would be to use indirect dynamic belays with multiple anchor points whenever possible. It is important also to have a secure stance so that as much load as possible can be taken off the anchor points. One final point

-under certain conditions the climbing rope will become frozen and ice encrusted making the use of mechanical belay devices next to impossible. In this instance the waist belay through karabiners will have to be used.

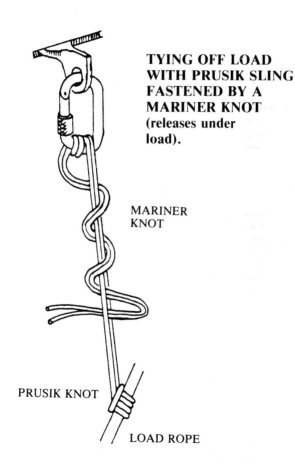

TYING OFF LOAD WITH PRUSIK SLING FASTENED BY A MARINER KNOT (releases under load).

MARINER KNOT

PRUSIK KNOT

LOAD ROPE

TYING OFF AN ITALIAN HITCH WITH HALF HITCH ON THE BIGHT
(Releases under load)

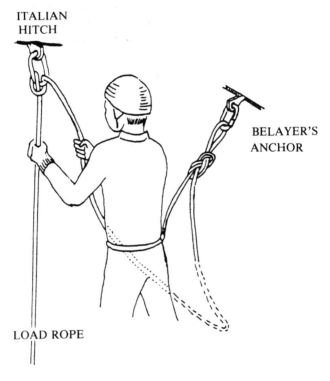

ITALIAN HITCH

BELAYER'S ANCHOR

LOAD ROPE

DIRECT BELAY USING AN ITALIAN HITCH
BELAYER ON SEPARATE ANCHOR

Protection and Running Belays on Ice

The primary function of the running belay is to protect the leader in the event of a fall by reducing the distance he descends. The severity of a fall is measured by the FALL FACTOR: This is obtained by dividing the length of the fall by the length of rope run out. e.g. A climber leading out 20 feet of rope placing no running belays falls 40 feet giving a fall factor of 2. (40/20). This is the maximum fall factor and is reached everytime whatever distance the climber falls up to the full length of the rope if he does not place any running belays. Although the severity of a fall is constant the longer the fall the longer the impact time. e.g. the longer the force acts on the belay chain. Therefore, falls should be kept as short as possible. The introduction of the running belay into the climbing chain has dramatic effects on the fall factor and the impact time. Both are reduced. A climber leading out 20 feet and falling off having placed a runner at 10 feet, experiences a fall of 20 feet and a fall factor of 1 (20/20). He falls only 20 feet rather than 40 feet and the impact time is correspondingly reduced.

1. The First Runner Rule is to place a runner as soon as it is feasible after setting out from the stance and belay. As a general rule the harder and steeper the climb the greater the propensity to use runners. In practice it is advisable to runner up in the easier climbs as well, as there is more likelihood of injury during a fall in the more broken easy climb than on vertical walls.

A modern (11mm) climbing rope is designed to absorb the energy generated by the fall and to have an impact force of 1200. This is the maximum impact force the belayer will be subjected to. However, when a runner is introduced into the system it is subjected to double the impact force

$$2 \times 1200 \text{ Kg.} = 2400 \text{ Kg. (5280 lbs.)}$$

The heaviest load through the system is therefore placed on the running belay and consequently, the Second Runner Rule is:

2. The runners should be capable of withstanding twice the maximum impact force 2400 Kg. whenever possible. In practice, dynamic belaying, rope friction, and knot slippage absorb some of the energy and this force is rarely fully exerted on the running belay. However, in the runner chain there should always be some full strength runners.

3. The Third Basic Runner Rule is that the components of the runner chain - the sling or rope, the knot and the karabiner should be

of uniform strength as the strength of the runner is the strength of its weakest link.

*N.B. The maximum holding power of an ice screw is 2000 Kg. in good ice!

Ethical Considerations of Runner Placement

Having established the basic rules governing runners the question arises, how many should you use and when should you place them, The number of ice screw runners carried and used on a pitch depends on personal preference and availability of placement on the climb. Assuming a runner interval of 20 feet on very steep ice 8 ice screws in a 160ft pitch would appear to be reasonable. It is possible to over protect a pitch and one should avoid the tendency to 'screw up' a pitch in order to compensate for lack of technical competence and confidence. Within the current ethical framework a running belay (ice screw) is for protection only although five stages of usage can be distinguished.

1. Protection - conventional use
2. Resting - clipping in and resting on a tight rope
3. Tension - used as partial aid to complete a move
4. Direct Aid - used directly to assist upward progress'
5. Point of Retreat - when unable to complete the pitch. May also be used in conjunction with the Yoyo technique - alternate leads of same pitch placing progressively higher runners until the pitch is overwhelmed by this joint effort.

Dynamic Consideration of Runner Placement

The climber must give consideration to his direction of fall when he places a runner and also the resulting direction of pull on the seond. If the lead climber has climbed up and traversed to the side and then placed a runner then the direction of pull will be diagonally up and the belayer should change his position accordingly. If this is not done there is a danger of the belayer being pulled off his stance if it is a small one and even being injured by being pulled against projecting rock. Care should be exercised when belaying in natural sentry boxes and alcoves. It is essential that the belay anchors be multi-directional.

Rope Drag on Long Pitches

This may be minimized by the following:-

1. Use the double rope technique - double 8mm or double 9mm.
2. Place runners in as straight a line as possible.
3. Extend each ice screw runner with a tape sling.

Anchor Points for Running Belays

In line with clean climbing practices the less the environmental impact the greater the acceptability of the anchor points. This must be tempered with the maintenance of an acceptable safety level. Applying this criteria it is possible to compile the following list:

1. Natural Anchors
2. Chocks
3. Rock Pitons
4. Ice Screws
5. Bolts

I have placed rock pitons ahead of ice screws because of greater potential holding power. The use of bolts as runners is really an interesting discussion point and is generally only found on climbs with thin ice which precludes the placement of screws as protection. eg. The classic Bourgeau Left Hand in the Rocky Mountains of Canada.

APPENDIX A:
GRADING OF SNOW AND ICE CLIMBS

The grading of snow and ice climbs is still an area of some discussion, however, it is generally agreed that the Scottish Grading System rating climbs from I to V using Roman numerals is the most acceptable. Both Albi Sole in Canada and Jeff Lowe in the United States have used the Scottish system as the basic system with the former adding a Grade VI and the latter combining it with the Yosemite Decimal system. The Canadian Grading System is reproduced here.

Grade I   Short straightforward snow or ice slope up to 50°.

Grade II   Either a short climb with some easy technical ice or a longer climb with some short technical steps.

Grade III   A more serious undertaking which may take several hours and include longer pitches of moderate ice between 70°-80°. Or the climb may be short and quite steep.

Grade IV   Includes similar but longer difficulties to those found on Grade III climbs. Or the climbs may be short but technically very difficult.

Grade V   A long climb with sustained technical difficulties.

Grade VI   A technically difficult and serious undertaking which may include the logistic problems of winter alpine climbing, avalanche danger, high elevation and remoteness. Will often take two-three days to complete.

Lately the trend in winter climbing development in Britain has been onto the steeper, vertical and overhanging, rock buttresses. By their very nature these tend to hold less snow and ice. As a result the routes involve a greater proportion of rock climbing than the older style snow and ice routes. Consequently since 1991 the Scottish system has expanded to include a two-tier system. The aim being to grade mixed routes, indicating their high levels of technical difficulty, whilst also catering for the more straightforward pure ice routes which may be technically easier though more serious.

Whilst Roman numerals still indicate the overall difficulty of the climb, accompanying Arabic numerals indicate the level of technical difficulty found on the hardest section of the route. A V,5 can be taken as an average grade V route. A higher technical grade than the overall grade (V,6) indicates greater technical difficulty offset by better protection. A lower technical grade (V,4) indicates greater seriousness. Arabic numerals are generally applied from grade IV upwards.

It should be remembered that the 'Grade' is only an indication since climbing conditions can vary considerably according to snow depth, type and thickness of ice and temperature and one will find variations within the grading conditions. 'Good' and 'Bad' conditions will alter grades and in the latter case may make a climb impossible or extremely dangerous. The climber must also consider avalanche, ice collapse, rock fall, white outs, hypothermia and frostbite as attendant environmental hazards which can affect all grades of climbs and climbers.

APPENDIX B: CONDITIONS

The ice climber should develop an awareness for ice conditions - colour, texture, hardness and temperature are all clues to ice quality.

Colour can provide the first clue to ice conditions.

Opaque ice is often soft.

Grey colour is an indication of thin or hollow ice.

Clear ice is an indication of new ice and indicates brittleness.

Blue/Green is a sign of older ice and generally good ice for climbing and screw placement.

The prevailing temperature will also be an important factor in determining ice conditions - very low temperatures cause the ice to be hard and brittle, temperatures above freezing produce soft slushy ice with poor screw placements, temperatures just below freezing are ideal for ice climbing.

There are several other forms of ice the climber may encounter:

Rime Ice   This is caused by water droplets freezing on a surface exposed to wind. These deposits grow to windward and can be solid enough to climb on under certain conditions.

Hoarfrost   This is caused by the sublimation of water vapour from the atmosphere onto a solid surface - rock, trees and even people.

Verglas   This is a thin coating of ice sheeting rock rather like the black ice we find on our highways in winter. It is caused by:

1.   Freezing rain on rock.
2.   Wet rock subject to freezing temperatures.
3.   Freezing fog.

Verglas makes climbing extremely difficult and crampons have to be worn even on the easiest grades of rock climbs.

Firnspeigel This is a thin layer of ice which forms just below the surface on snowfields in the spring. Once formed it provides a greenhouse effect and the snow underneath the ice skin melts. Under certain conditions i.e. strong enough ice skin, firnspeigel can provide excellent climbing conditions.

APPENDIX C: ICE FORMATION AND TYPES

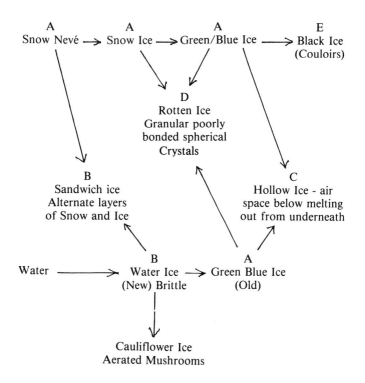

CLIMBABILITY
A = Good
B = Fair - protection poor
C = Delicate
D = Poor
E = Difficult - Tough Ice